Gerald Locklin

Poets and Pleasure Seekers

New and Selected Poems
2010 – 2015

First Edition

March 2015

Text Copyright ©2015 by Gerald Locklin
Foreword Copyright ©2015 by Alexis Rhone Fancher
Cover Art Copyright ©2015 by Ann Brantingham
Author Photo Copyright ©2015 by Alexis Rhone Fancher

All Rights Reserved.

Please contact the author for permissions at
gerlocklin@gmail.com

www.spouthillpress.com
Pomona, California

ISBN-13: 978-0692388198

ISBN-10: 0692388192

for

*Ann and John Brantingham:
In gratitude for their many years
of Unwavering Friendship and Loyal Support*

Foreword

I've got a thing for Gerald Locklin's poems. He zeros in on the heart of life and won't let go. I especially love his ekphrastic poems, and there's a feast of them in this new collection. Everyone from Dürer to Diebenkorn. I couldn't help but slip into Locklin's "slide," a luscious tribute to Miles, Coltrane, Dix, and Bird. And don't get me started on those tender love poems to his wife, camouflaged as ekphrastic homage. I'd call them worshipful if they weren't so damn human.

Then there are those "less lofty" poems. The ones about everything from birth to death and all the messy stuff in between. The poems that celebrate weddings, exercise, the vagaries of love and sex, professorial woes, the mixed blessings of aging, the joyous birth of a grandchild are each grounded in Locklin's singular Long Beach aesthetic, each universal in its appeal.

Me? I like the erotic poems best. No one writes sex like Gerald Locklin. The unabashed maleness of his poems knocks me out every time. "My wet dreams are getting drier/but awake I can shoot down every aircraft/How damp are a woman's humid dreams?" ("Lola Alvarez Bravo: *El sueño del ahogado*, c. 1945.") I love that Locklin has an ongoing love affair with the female of the species. A self-professed "leg man," he celebrates his erotic proclivities.

What else to say except the brilliant force of nature that is my dear friend, Gerald Locklin, has done it again. Produced a book of such truth and beauty, such self-deprecating humor and wit, such inclusiveness, that it has stayed with me long after I devoured every page. "I am a musician of the English Language," Toad says in "The Toad Solution." Believe it.

-Alexis Rhone Fancher, author of *How I Lost My Virginity To Michael Cohen & Other Heart Stab Poems*, poetry editor of *Cultural Weekly*.

Table of Contents

paul cézanne: *the alle at chantilly*, 1888	13
albrecht dürer: *adam and eve*, 1504	14
richard diebenkorn: *freeway and snapshot*, 1957	15
hans-christian schink: *autobahn landscape*, photograph	16
Willem de Kooning: *Pink Angels*, 1945	17
slide	18
The Winter Trees of Summer	20
Andy Warhol: *A Boy for Me*, 1962	21
Today's Avant-Garde go over the Hill Tomorrow	22
Lorenzo Lotto: *Venus and Cupid*	23
Giovanni di Paolo: *The Expulsion of Adam and Eve from Paradise*	24
David Hockney: *Lithograph of Water Made of Thick and Thin Lines, a Green Wash, a Light Blue Wash and a Dark Blue Wash (Pool 1)*, 1978-80, Lithograph in Seven Colors	25
John Singleton Copley: *Portrait of Elizabeth Ross (Mrs. William Tyng)*, 1766	26
Rembrandt: *The Polish Rider*, 1655	27
Eileen Agar: *Ladybird*, 1936	28
Lauren Simonutti: *Bring the Candle to the Flame*, Slipstream Postcard	29
Karet Taipei: *Collage #45*, 1938	30
Lola Alvarez Bravo: *El sueño del ahogado*, c. 1945	31
"Giant Steps," "Countdown," and "Spiral"	32
Harmonizing over the Bar Lines	33
Frida Kahlo: *Mi vestigo cuelga ahi (My dress hangs there)*, 1933	35
Cindy Sherman: *Untitled #123*, 1983	36
he reads; she beads	37
those people who call other people paranoid	38
Agustin Lazo: *The Family Reunion*, ca. 1931	39
Matisse: *Le Bonheur de Vivre*, 1905-06	40
Eugene Berman: *Hugh and Bridget Chisholm*, 1940	41

Lola Alvarez Bravo: *El sueño del ahogado (The Dream of the Drowned)*	42
The Unicorn in Captivity, Brussels, 1495-1505	43
Double Call, photo, Nilserik Larson, *Slipstream*, #33	44
Memories of Madness, photograph by Andrea Faseni, Front Cover, *Slipstream #33*	45
Grand Designs and Delusions of Grandeur	46
Picasso: *Le Moulin de la Galette*, Winter 1900	47
Picasso: *Woman Ironing*	48
Honoré Daumier: *The Laundress*, 1863	49
Sir Anthony VanDyck: *Marchesa Giovanna Cattaneo*	50
Fast and Furious	51
"Naima" and "A Love Supreme"	52
Those Who Drive the Engine	53
Incomparability	54
Helen Lundeborg: *Plant and Animal Analogies*, 1934-35	55
something to hang on to	56
Make Of This What You Will	58
who's who	59
the common reader	60
John Hoppner: *The Ladies Sarah and Catherine Bligh*, circa 1790	62
Jackson Pollock: *Untitled*, 1945	63
a teacher's idea of paradise	64
henry's gift	65
changing of the guard	67
the missing ingredient	68
A Still from *Diary of a Country Priest*	70
Bun Eater, photo, Nilserik Larson, *Slipstream*, #33	71
an item from manila	72
ancient music	73
timing is everything	74
the lyrics linger on	75
I Give Up, or I Want My Sixty Bucks Back	77
Grand-Madonna and Child	78
No Free Lunch	80
Francis Picabia: *Alarm Clock*, 1919	81
The Toad Solution	82

Huxley's Soma	83
My Fifteen Seconds of Fame	84
Olfactory Poetics	85
The Wedding of Tyler and Nicole	86
A Formerly Omniscient Toad	87
The Consequences of Childhood/Adolescent Deprivations	88
Grace Plethorpe: *Ancestors, II*, 1935, Ink	89
A Momentary Mental Lapse	90
No Green Berlin	91
A Green Thought?	94
The Secret to My Success	95
the silence	96
Orthographic Depths in Secret Gardens	97
Cryptography	98
Who the hell greenlighted it?	99
Nothing Special Anymore	100
From Gloat to Goat	101
Thumbnail Guide for the Senior Couplers	102
I Hate Hollywood	103
Gustave Moreau: *Oedipus and the Sphinx*, 1864	105
Dieric Bouts: *Virgin and Child*, 1455-60	106
Camille Pisarro: *The Garden of the Tuileries on a Spring Morning*, 1899	107
Colum Colvin: *Cupid and Psyche*, 1986	108
Vincent Van Gogh: *The Flowering Orchard* and Claude Monet: *Fruit Trees in Blossom*	109
Maybe at Heart	110
Pablo Picasso: *Seated Harlequin*, 1901	111
Henri Matisse: *Icarus*, Plate Vii of *Jazz*, 1947	112
Paul Cézanne: *Still Life with a Ginger Jar and Eggplants*, 1893-94	113
Hippopotamus: Egypt	114
Filippino Lippi: *Madonna and Child*, 1483-84	115
"Doctor, I want a lens I can trust!"	116
Vincent Van Gogh: *Irises*, 1890	117
George Woodall: *Vase*, late 19th Century	118

Constantin Guys: *Young Woman in a Blue and*
  Black Dress — 119
The Kindest Cut — 120
Andy Warhol: *Nice Jackies*, 1964 — 121
Diego Rivera: *The Flower Carriers*, 1935 — 122
a pathetic finale — 123
Robert Colescott: *End of the Trail*, 1976 — 124

paul cézanne: *the alle at chantilly,* 1888

now we return to that house which
we left so many centuries ago.
the trees have learned a subtler music,
less of grimm or notre dame,
and more of gawain's chapel.
the mansard roofs are gray as northern
seas, the slate of quarries that we
visited in wales above caernarvon and
the lleyn peninsula. god makes a tree-
trunk, while man carves a wooden barrier,
shin-high, across the overgrown approach,
buildings now will always co-exist with
forests, and a window's boards will
shutter or accede as air or nocturne
dictate. It will be there waiting for
us, empty as a symphony, as arches
accolade and arcades guillotine, and
willows weep for everyone but thee.

albrecht dürer: *adam and eve,* 1504

she has a face that would stop
a serpent in its serpentine tracks.
in fact, she has a beak on her
that strongly resembles that of
the bird on adam's branch.
she'd have to be the only lay
in town to stand a chance of
getting me to taste a fruit
that's already been in a snake's mouth.

and as if it weren't going to be
punishment enough for adam,
in exile with her somewhere east
of eden, and no flags yet invented
to pull over her head and fuck for
old glory,

it looks to me as if
the fig leaf he's selected for
this crucial day's attire

may be poison ivy.

richard diebenkorn: *freeway and snapshot,* **1957**

the aqueduct flows
free and blue, downhill,
a little or a lot, but
so does everything: the
grass flows green and
greener, and the slopes
flow sloppier and sloppiest,
but never sloppily. the
gravel flows like shale or
scree because the other side
of an embankment's always
greener. the bridges flow in
both directions, bank to
bank, like greenback whales.

the forest flows until the
day the sheriff of nothingness
arrests its cardiacal sap. the
easement flows in case a
horse or bicycle or highwayman
should happen by.

lines are drawn, though,
like a hundred-dollar haircut.
no flow flows into another.

i can't discern a freeway.

hans-christian schink: *autobahn landscape*, photograph

nothing's more concrete than concrete.
nothing's less flat that a flatland.
ozone is as odorless as jesus.

relegate the barnyard to the
intersection of the land and sky.
push the people off the edge.
varnish the vanishing point.

untramelled autobahn from
everywhere to nowhere.
altar of discontinuities.
glacial psalm.

stonehenge, oxymandias, obelisk.
salt of the earth.
oblong edifice of imperturbability.

pillar of patience.
featureless rosetta stone.
testament to space and time.

satire has the shortest shelf-life.

romanticism has not left a footprint.

Willem de Kooning: *Pink Angels*, 1945

This may be the only pink thing –
Other than female nipples and lips,
Above or below
(And lipstick on either is a redundant
Perversity) that has ever held the least interest
Or attraction for me. Why is it an exception?
Because this early masterpiece demonstrates
That the artist had already schooled himself
In the works of his predecessors: all
Of them of all historical periods in
Western Art, which had already before him
Appropriated the Asian, African, and American
Indian signature traits and symbolic traditions.
T.S. Eliot summed up the relationship of
Tradition to the Individual Talent in the 1920s.
But he is too erudite and, on the surface, difficult
For the young to stand up to. It's easier to dismiss
Him with ridicule and extraneous political
Considerations: the refuges of ignorance.
It's their loss, and they are no loss to us
Who have made the effort, as de Kooning did,
To welcome into the viscous optical gel of the
Imagination the flotation of pink angels that suggest
Platonic Form and Modern Ingenuity.

slide

the early days of be-bop
were before my time,
but listening to the great trombonist,
a slightly second-generation protégé
of bird and diz and bud,
now master to a new generation
of young turks, you realize that
joy was the essence of it,
playing fast and furious and
changing streetcars on the run,
the unadulterated fun of it,
the jet-age waiting on the runway,
the new-found freedoms grafted onto
roots of field songs, blues, and
spirituals, and the urban voyage of
discovery up and down the black and white
keys of the mississippi—
n'orlins, st. louis, chicago—
spreading wings then east to harlem,
west to central avenue,
rites of passage back across both oceans,
sheer excitement of the opening up of it,
the glimpses of untold possibilities,
the scalding chill of what infinity might be.

miles and monk and chet and coltrane—
they'd usher in a different consciousness,
postwar parisian existentialism,
journey inward,
exploration of the self,
the symphony of mind,
search for the elusive blue note,
the <u>ineffable</u> of mallarmé and baudelaire,
the chordal confrontation with resurgence
of a life lived only once,
the intimation that this freedom

was an all, an everything, an
inescapable condition, something
from which there was no retreat
but only the totality of an
evolving orchestration,
the supreme love,
darkness at each end of it.

in the days before the war, though,
in the days when america refused
to be depressed by a depression,
there was confirmation of
the ornithology
of the unorthodox,
an escalation, exhalation,
expectation, exaltation.

doesn't matter how young bird died—
read walter pater,
read the life of christ.

jazz is about origins and endings,
which, as that aficionado of cool cats,
tom eliot, discovered in a gardened, country
churchyard, hewn upon the mossy stones,
are one.

The Winter Trees of Summer
For the Irishman Joyce and the Welshman Thomas

On Radnor Avenue, one block away,
The trees have not forgotten the unforeseeable frost,
Although the days at last are warming.
The municipal arborists arbitrarily decreed that this year
A severe trim was in order all the way up to
Their willowy, widowy peaks,
Reducing their Wagnerian tufts to Mozartian muppets
That used to bend as shady canopy, arcade, chapel or
Bishop's arch-nave the length of the thoroughfare,
Within our tract, like baobabs or jacarandas,
Though my wife insists they are not either,
Are a species with which she is not familiar,
Maybe gardened by the Brothers Grimm.
Their branches now, thick as anacondas,
Dance their horizontal, giant, yogurt-yaughust,
Almost oaken, salamander-gray-great-graynesses
That bear not fruit or nuts or bombast,
Just the threat of nightmarish, Ovidian,
Asphyxiating, beddy-bye, annihilating hugs
To cars, homes, women, children, pets, planets
And would-be SuperDuperHeroes. Our leaders tried to play
Dum-dum-Dalilas to their Samsonite Thuggage,
While taxes, Abraxas, and Iran distracted us.
They will limply drop us down the limpid walls of wells
Of pothole loneliness into Hell's Lethean, oblisionary
Looping Lena's Leap.

Andy Warhol: *A Boy for Me,* 1962

Never underestimate Andy!

For some reason it never occurred to me,
Until I read it in the National Gallery Guide Book,
That this tabloid page of the New York Post,
Heralding Sinatra and the Rat Pack,
As well as the Royal Birth
(And weather and stock prices)
Was not a silkscreen, but had been
Painted by hand.
(I did not know that he had started out as
A commercial illustrator, (of, especially,
Shoes)).

And let's not forget that no one
So forcefully predicted our current national
Obsession with "Reality" entertainment
Than Andy, with his fixation upon celebrity
Status, and his perpetuation of the myth of
Celebrity "Immortality."

Tell me: Is any phrase more quoted
In our age of Anonymous Idols than Andy's
"Fifteen minutes of Fame?"

No, never underestimate sly ol'
Androgynously nerdy,
Disarmingly powerful
Andy,

And his craftily Self-Fulfilling
Prophesies.

Today's Avant-Garde go over the Hill Tomorrow

Harry Cooper, the curator of the exhibition
Of the Meyerhoff Collection, a donation to
The National Gallery of Art,
Divided the show and his catalog essay
Into ten logical topics, the second of which
Was concentricity.

Kenneth Noland's *Mandarin*, for instance, borrows
The notion of Josef Albers' *Homage to the Square*
For his acrylic of concentric circles. Frank Stella's
Gray Scrabble is a more obvious optical
Arrangement of boxes with boxes. His
Marquis de Portago is similarly symmetrical,
As are his untitled half-circles.

It was Josef Albers, however, who anticipated
The poststructuralist de-centering of the human,
History, and the self, as his squares began to move
Towards the margins. Richard Serra roughed
The edges of his swirls; Jasper Johns curled up
The corners of his mirrors, flags, and windows;
Ellsworth Kelly gave wings to his *Red Curve*;
And Robert Rauschenberg's brilliant
Autobiography surveyed his aesthetic evolution
Through the triptych of Da Vinci,
The pop-and-personal, and techno-cybernetic
Space flight. And as the marginalized took
Center stage, the world within the consciousness
Turned inside-out, and things fell apart,
As Yeats and Achebe always knew they would.

Lorenzo Lotto: *Venus and Cupid*

The Goddess of Love is dangling with right hand
A myrtle wreath as blessing of marriage. The
Countenance of the bride has been bestowed
Upon the goddess, whose body may also
Have been homage to the Human. It is amply
Favored by breasts whose nipples tempt even their
Owner to excite. A similarly coquettish tummy
Serves as canopy to a composite of labia and petals.
If this, a torso braiding, and a remarkably well-turned
Ankle, are not sufficiently sensuous to turn us on
Five centuries hence, we have the ambivalent comedy
Of Cupid's peeing through a ring of laurel onto her
"Lap." His little dick, surprisingly long, his laugh
Both innocently childish and paternally dominating,
Perhaps anticipates the substitution of her slender
Finger for his chubby one. Were Cupids, I wonder,
Born to their role or did they require the wine, olive
Oil, and tea-leaves of sympathy of actual or surrogate
Mothers? And how many couples still today, I wonder,
Employ the levity of urine as refreshing variation from
The Gravitas of Holy Water?

Giovanni di Paolo: *The Expulsion of Adam and Eve from Paradise*

Are these the smallest breasts ever painted?
She only has Adam beat by about a centimeter.
The prettiest, cutest woman I ever fell in love with
Seemed, clothed, flat-chested beneath her blouse.
I have never gazed upon more exquisite facial features,
Though, a product of a European melting pot heredity,
And the most flawlessly shaped legs a leg-man such as I
Could ever have desired. Then, removing the silk,
I uncovered apples that would have proved Adam's undoing.
I used to rise up over her and fight to restrain myself from
Coming at the very sight of what I'd conquered. We still
Sleep in the same bed going on fifty years of unmitigated
Wars and mutual betrayals, and she has aged less
Than any woman you will ever meet—she's worked at
That, but so did generations of heredities, a revenge
Of the flesh, were I to succumb to begging for it.

David Hockney: *Lithograph of Water Made of Thick and Thin Lines, a Green Wash, a Light Blue Wash and a Dark Blue Wash (Pool 1)*, **1978-80, Lithograph in Seven Colors**

Well, he's certainly done the job of
Describing the damn thing for me.
And I read in the catalogue,
A New World Imagined: Art of the Americas,
Of social phenomena I have observed myself
In the Santa Monica and Hollywood adjacent to
The Long Beach where I've lived for fifty years now:
The fluidity, "special relationship," and comfort
Of dual residences enjoyed by British and American
Artists from the nineteenth century of John Singer Sargent
To my own lifetime of Auden, Spender, and Hockney,
That intuitive affinity that Churchill and Roosevelt
Remarked upon, solidified by the two world wars
Of the twentieth century, to the extent that scholars
Debate the primary inspirational landscapes:
Yorkshire Hills or Mulholland Drive.

What stands out, though, is the essential freedom
Of movement and association cherished by the two nations,
And fought for side-by-side (these two people—what a
Brilliant phrase: "Separated by a common language.")

For a while our public broadcasting system abandoned
The British television imports it had thrived on
In favor of "multiculturalism," and just about went broke
Doing so. Now multiple American cultures once again
Get to enjoy the Brits' masterpieces, history, and wry sense of humor.
And even I, thrice almost killed by London, and Irish of heritage,
Keep returning to the graveyards I once drank my breakfast in,
And to revivals of Pinter and Stoppard and Synge and,
The Irish-American O'Neill,
Back in the USA,
On Broadway.

John Singleton Copley: *Portrait of Elizabeth Ross (Mrs. William Tyng)*, 1766

"Ross," indeed: Hair, eyelids, lips, and robe
All partake of the pallet of redness, from russet to
Shimmering rose. Her breasts require no support
Beyond the limp bodice through which
Her liberated nipples beckon. The triangular
Strength of face and chin is modulated into
Sensuality by the happily complicit countenance,
While a winged symbol of conquest perches on a
Finger and lusts to nibble at her mouth.
The grip of the other hand upon the sumptuous
Silks suggests the ease with which they could be
Lifted to reveal the uncorseted folds of a
Coyly receptive woman. Hers is a beauty
That delivers what it promises.

A New World Imagined: Art of the Americas
Traces the lineage of the style "Turquerie"
From the Near East via the England and Europe of
Lady Mary Wortley Montagu's *Letters*
To the newly wealthy of America, proud of their
Acquisitions of a past. We were to be the melting pot
Not merely of nationalities, but of their various
Embodiments of the Platonic Idea of the Beautiful.

To which I cry, "Hurrah, Huzzah, the More the Merrier . . .
Just keep 'em coming!

And they do.

Rembrandt: *The Polish Rider,* 1655

So this is where this famous painting is stabled:
At Henry Frick's house,
Though it's ridden forth on loan to
More museums than the miles
The Polish Rider himself rode.

Still, no one had definitively
Interpreted it. Maybe it just means
Whatever it means to each of us,
Since Mr. van Rijn inconveniently
(For us) forgot to leave word
What it meant to him.

To me, today, as I sit writing uneasily
In my easy chair,
It means the enduring, restless spirit
Of the friends I have known
Of Polish or similar "Extractions,"
Those of Central or Eastern Europe:
Edward Field and Ed Ochester,
Dave and Phil Alvin, the Cherins,
Two Vollmers, the Weinbergs,
Dave Newman, Lori Jakiela,
All whose ancestors hailed from Central Europe,
Eastern Europe, the whole damn Burgh of Pitt,
The bruising basketball team of Holy Redeemer Parish,
Back when cities were divided not on racial grounds,
So much as by religions/nationalities.
Let me raise a phantom (but real-potato) vodka
To you, or a virtual boilermaker.
You rode the white horse with the charging gait
Across the oceans to produce the fruited plains,
Extract the minerals for the machines,
And build The House of Song and of the Intellect.

Eileen Agar: *Ladybird*, 1936

Finally, I don't place much credence
In any theory of universal, archetypal symbols
That play leapfrog in our unconscious minds,
And, when utilized as objects depicted
In art or referred to in poetry,
Speak from our psychic depths directly
To each other.

But I'll admit that the shadows, scribbles,
Stars, dials, wheels, ladybugs,
And the diaphanous wrapping,
Which partly obscure the naked woman
In the photograph, do fetishize her abnormality
And desirability kilowatts beyond that of any
Stripper in the carnivals and county fairs
Supposed to tantalize the panting, staring,
Google-eyed, but ultimately disappointed
Adolescents of my 1950s summers.

Then again, my son says that my art poems
Fall into two categories: those of women
I would "do," and those of women that
I "wouldn't."

This one I would definitely "do,"
In spite of her swollen knees
And a-symmetrical tits, but only if the
Illusory halogen remained an interface
'Twixt our deformities.

Lauren Simonutti: *Bring the Candle to the Flame*, Slipstream Postcard

It's three-quarters of a birthday cake,
Minus the wedge of chocolate flour
Sliced out of it, with nine or ten candles
Aflame atop the thick white frosting,
With the hand of a tattooed or shadowed arm
Clenched aside it in anticipation of sharp pain,
An ample breast extended towards
The highest, hottest flame,
The nipple half-exposed to it,
A human moth about to fuel and feed
The fire.

The woman's eyes are shut;
Her lips are tightened,
Hair and dress simple black,
A futuristic heroine of 1950s cinematic lust,
Born to draw boys and men to her bosom,
Seeking now the ultimate in sensual intensity
The re-birth of self-immolation:

And we're privileged to witness it
And weld the purity of our pain
To hers.

Karet Taipei: *Collage #45,* 1938

Bondage, amputation, impotence,
And effigy, surveilled by
The Extraterrestrial Maiden.

Surreal sexuality attempts
To neuter with absurdity
The guilt-ridden cruelty
That Bataille identified
As a primordial human craving.

Oh Cosmeticological Mannequin!
We will rescue and embrace you
As limbless, cinematic Mona Lisa,
Before recommencing the torturing
Of what is left of you.

Lola Alvarez Bravo: *El sueño del ahogado,* c. 1945

Ambiguities haunt our languages
Of dream, desire, figuration.
Are there little quince princesses
Posing upon the river, fallen branches,
Rocks, and diving-board pilings—
The inhabitants of the slumbering Head
Of the decapitated, recapitated Orpheus,
Or is he the handsome cynosure
Of their collective virginal lust.

Do we meet our Incubi and Succubi
In the colorless weather of the night?
Are we allowed to remember
Our silver seductions
In monochromatic flashbacks,
Or do they only remain as muscle memory.

My wet dreams are getting drier,
But awake I can shoot down every aircraft.

How damp are a woman's humid dreams?

"Giant Steps," "Countdown," and "Spiral"

Clearly, Coltrane visualized his melodies
As figures sketched upon the scales.
So did Miles and Bill Evans
In the modular *Kind of Blue*,
And Brubeck in the titles of *Time Out*:
e.g. "Take Five" and "Blue Rondo a la Turk."

Especially, though, Miles and Gil Evans
In the chromatics, in both senses,
Of *Sketches of Spain*.

Harmonizing over the Bar Lines

As the beneficiary of so many gifts
Of Jazz CDs from the brilliant Swedish
Watercolorist, Poet (in English!), and raconteur,
Henry Denander, I had absorbed a few
Of the keys (pun intended) to the genius
Of Bill Evans that had led Miles Davis
To replace the legendary Red Garland with Bill
In a combo that was to produce a string
Of masterpieces. I understood the concept
Of multiple simultaneous improvising within
A trio, rather than the traditional series of solos,
But it has only been while listening to
The two-CD set, *Live at Art D'Lugoff's Top of
The Gate*, that I began to *hear* what the right hand
Was doing over the left, the quasi-melodic
Extended runs of the right, over the independently
Mnemonic chords of the left. It was as if I were
Listening to two pianistic geniuses at facing
Baby grands, dueling with two overlapping
Styles of artistry. This was probably grade-school
Stuff to Henry, but it had taken me decades of
Aural-mental widening to grasp this multi-tasking
Mastery. Now I could just sit back and enjoy.

I had been suffering from headaches similar to
The ones that have afflicted Henry for years,
From which he seeks solace and inspiration
On his Greek island. He's invited me over,
But I just can't get there right now. So he somehow
Devised this musical transportation and transformation
Of gray matter as a substitute island to counter
These years in which the clock speeds up,
And the person slows down. Nor has he abandoned
The consolations of the old-fashioned handwritten
Letter, enclosed in an envelope decorated and
Personalized by a multi-talented mind.

He can still, like another old friend,
The world-renowned environmental physicist,
Gary Sposito—the most literate scientist
I've ever known—with the hand-eye coordination
Of a medieval monk—craft a letter from one friend
To another, that not only does the intended trick,
But is actually worth preserving,
On multiple counts,
For posterity.

Thanks, pal, for the dual gift of
Friendship and of spherical, celestial music,
The kind designed to soothe
The savage, self-destructive brain.

Frida Kahlo: *Mi vestigo cuelga ahi (My dress hangs there),*
1933

It's a collage of a cast of thousands
And world of places,
And dictionary of objects
That had gone into her inner life
In recent years, and there's a poignancy
Of betrayal unifying them.

But they're spatially arranged
And do not attempt
The stream of narrative consciousness.
So they don't tell us everything
Though maybe Frida *and* Virginia Woolf
Together could.
Or Joyce, Stein, and Picasso.
Or Hemingway, Faulkner, and Cezanne.

The cinema tries to
And fails.

But the darn thing does demonstrate
The stature of her talent,
Though her heart may have silenced
Her sense.

It definitely demonstrates
(Demon strates?)
That the mind is awfully effing
Cluttered.

Cindy Sherman: *Untitled #123*, 1983

MOMA says this "chromogenic color print . . .
"Parodies the mannerisms of
Codified female beauty
Championed in fashion ads
By mimicking their appeal."

All I know is that both the parody and
The fashion ads that the parody is
Ostensibly parodying still retain
Their appeal for me.

So fuck you, Cindy.

he reads; she beads

to a writer of his generation
silence is golden; thus,
how his heart sinks
whenever she says,

"put something on the t.v.,
please, whatever you want. i
just need a little background
noise."

those people who call other people paranoid

are sometimes qualified psychiatrists
who know the difference between
psychosis and legitimate fears,
sensible cautions,

but more often they are those
who would rather not know that
they have few secrets, little safety,

or do not want *you* to.

Agustin Lazo: *The Family Reunion,* ca. **1931**

I guess the woman in floor-length white gown
Spanking the plump bottom of a child
Is the Mother, and that the little man
In a proper suit and tie, holding a globe,
While studying some maps, is the first son,
Preparing for or reminiscing upon the
Colonial voyage from which he has just
Triumphantly returned, and that the apparent
Daughter, whining shrewfully, reaches in vain
For the world, but seems destined for
The Motherhood of the naked, ape-like Younger
Brother, about to make passage from
The Imaginary Realm to the Symbolic.

Meanwhile, clad in skintight slacks, white shirt,
And slippers, He buries his head in the
News of the Day, or is, head on pillow, about to
Seek refuge in dozing off from it.

I guess this is an early Lacanian satire of the
Rigidity of gendered role-differentiation.
If so, the system had broken down in time
For a woman and her two female contributors
To edit the catalogue of *Drawing Surrealism*,
With its 240 pages and 200-plus illustrations.

Matisse: *Le Bonheur de Vivre*, 1905-06

The colors make each other move,
Upon the retinas, within the synapses.
The people are caught as absences,
Photographic negatives within the
Spectral flames. They are naked
As the supernatural. If Dante were
A Fauvist, this is how he would have
Crayoned the afterlife. The title
Is pleonastic as plasticity: To live
Is to be happy, because to be alive,
In this life, is itself a happiness.

And those who are not happy
Die. But that is for another
Canvas altogether, one of Munch's,
Perhaps, or Francis (that pig) Bacon's,
Or Lucien Freud's. In this Matisse,
And even in quick brushstrokes
Of Van Gogh, which persist within
A corner of Matisse, the best death
Is a visionary aneurism.

Eugene Berman: *Hugh and Bridget Chisholm*, 1940

The girlish rich husband adores
The auburn-tressed, red-lipped,
Cleft-chinned, sad-eyed woman.

The artist adored them both.
They were part of an international circle
Of married, cohabitating, gay, lesbian,
Heterosexual, British, American, French,
Mexican, supportive, misogynistic,
talented, and less so,
Individuals, Couples, and Serial
Anythings and Everythings.

That's the way artists are.
And were.
And weren't all Bohemians
Either.

So go ahead and generalize,
If it pleases you.
The wall placards at the exhibition
Are simplistically class-and-gender conscious,
But the catalogue's
Essays aren't.

Look at their artworks,
Clearly and long.
What are they trying to say to you?
Read my poems that way too, please.
Tell me what they tell you,
Not what you wish they did.
Don't put words in my mouth,
Or wash words out with soap.

Lola Alvarez Bravo: *El sueño del ahogado (The Dream of the Drowned)*

I assume the Dreamer is represented
By the male head floating in the river.
It is on its side and its lips are sealed—
Orpheus has been silenced.
(I used to have dreams of being
Rushed down a river current,
But it was not an altogether unpleasant sensation;
It was more like giving oneself over
To an amusement park ride,
Or being on a Bullet Train. And, anyway,
I haven't had the dream since I stopped drinking
And lost or alleviated my sleep apnea.)

The twelve (monthly) maidens
In identical white gowns and floral crowns
Do not seem overly concerned by the male's demise,
The End of the Male Gaze and the Male Voice.
Soon now the girls can begin to sing their own
Song and construct their own narratives.
Bye-bye, Loving Father/Daddy Warbucks.

It's such a beautiful work of art,
Such grace, such balance,
But is this how it has worked out
In the world away from the lithograph,
Or are the men still in power,
And the Empowered Women
Transmogrified into Men?

The Unicorn in Captivity, **Brussels, 1495-1505**

Please don't make me laugh with bullshit about
Christian Symbolism, legends, and the possible
Celebration of a marriage. Is that all they ever
Celebrated in the dawning from the dark ages:

Marriages? What a dark thing to celebrate—you
Never can catch me celebrating marriage, do you?
Can't you deconstruct the innocuous undermining of
The Super-Ego when you see it? Don't you
Feel the Libido subverting Respectability
With the tapering, potentially penetrating
Stiffness of the single horn—crowning glory
Of the bearded, thick-necked, handsome stallion—
Inadequately chained to a blossoming tree,
Pitifully circled by an enclosure of sticks,
Capable at any moment of vaulting free
To rampage o'er pacified field and forest?

The allegory is of that powerful beast, the Id,
Apt to smash both self and civilization to bits
At any willful moment.

The "Captivity" of the "Unicorn" is shown to be
A sham, a joke, a comforting delusion propagated
By Churches and Estates whose lawgivers prove the most
Prominent sinners against their own Commandments.

'Twas ever thus, and no less so today.

Double Call, photo, Nilserik Larson, *Slipstream*, #33

The silken blonde in the fetishistic undergarments
Invades the libidos of the tourist couple,
Both calling home to report
The utter but false joy of their honeymoon.
The new bride is a brunette and wears sunglasses,
Neither of them has gained a pound yet.
The rugged, somewhat scarred features
Of the groom still evoke a manliness
The young bride finds attractive.

The temptress, though not yet real
Is clearer to the eye than the couple or
Their reverse reflections in the showcase window
Of the upscale store from which their purchases
Will be delivered. She stretches and relaxes.
She is in no rush. Eventually she always wins
The man, the woman, their siblings, parents,
All of them.

Memories of Madness*, photograph by Andrea Faseni, Front Cover, *Slipstream #33

I do not enjoy photographs
Of rooms without a sexual woman to objectify,
But now I can sense the traces of the seductress
In this particular picture of a room
Without a person or a painting of one
In it.

Not just the blue ball of cushion
Shaped like an eyeless head,
But the slant of a cold winter light
That has not warmed the rumpled sheet of the bed yet;
The crumbling plaster of the walls and ceiling;
The practically open drawer
Of the moveable (medicine?) cabinet;
The moldy mattress extruding from beneath the pallet;
The thin wire encumbrances of the window frame;
The washed-out green of the garden leaves,
More like a diagonal rush of verticality,
Than a river of crushed lettuce.

Is this the attic of the Gilbert/Gubar *Madwoman?*
An above-ground dungeon?
The gothic past that haunts our hopes?
An awakening into Hamlet's nightmare:
Endless Being, freeze-framed.

Does this bear the Trace of Derrida?

The only answer to our prayers may be
The heaven that we never managed to imagine.

Grand Designs and Delusions of Grandeur

In the Half-World of Art
The former oft spawn the latter
Which nullify the former.

Picasso: *Le Moulin de la Galette*, **Winter 1900**

Masks and Ebony Mournings:
If God or Darwin had put smiles on faces,
The celebratory dissipation
Had undone them.

Picasso: *Woman Ironing*

Blue is about to vanish
Into the metaphysical and
Metaphorical Glare and Silence
Of Melville's Whale and Poe's Whiteout:

The nobility of honest labor decreases
As caloric intake succumbs
To malnutrition.

Honoré Daumier: *The Laundress*, 1863

The muscular and bent
Laundress and child,
Having achieved with their burdens
The top step of the stairway from
The bankside of the Seine,
Provide the naturalistic dark side
Of economic servitude
Prefatory to the gaiety of the Moulin Rouge,
And its raising of the skirts
Of Jane Avril and La Goulue,
And of the less storied Cancan Dancers
Of the posters of Toulouse-Lautrec,
Splitting naughtily their alabaster thighs
In hopes fairy-tale dukes and princes
Would empty their purses
Of a king's ransom of pleasure,
To bury their faces in womblike obliteration
Of any and all intimations
Of obese laundresses and their fatty offspring.

In a yet later time and place,
Poets and pleasure seekers
Came to The Cabaret.

Sir Anthony VanDyck: *Marchesa Giovanna Cattaneo*

Dear Mariacristina, My Seal,
Are you familiar with this painting?
From the photos you have sent me,
She is the "spitting image" of you,
Or vice-versa. That's a frontier
Americanism, but it means you have
The same curls and alert eyes
And reddish-brown hair, pert nose,
And witty lips. A strong upper body.
And a proud bearing. You could both
Stand up for yourselves. And since she was
From a distinguished Genoese family,
And you from Milan, also in the north,
You could be distantly related.

I don't know if you have ties to
Nobility of birth—I know I don't—
But you've already demonstrated
Meritocracy of mind and heart
And an ever-youthful loveliness.
But I'm not an artist.
You require Anthony VanDyck to capture
The uniqueness of your soul.

Fast and Furious

Sometimes Coltrane
Like Bird, Diz, and Bud,
Just wanted to see
How fast he could play.

That's okay too,
If you don't make a habit of it.

Coltane didn't,
And Miles didn't either.

Miles did the opposite.

"Naima" and "A Love Supreme"

Nat Hentoff calls it "The Cry,"
The explosive intent to express one's inner life
In one's music, art, or words.

The two are examples of the cry of love
For a soul-mate
And the cry of gratitude
To the Divine.

Both the lyric and the epic
Serve as avenues to the Transcendent.

Those Who Drive the Engine

It's said that a truly great athlete
Makes those around him better,
Maybe even brings out from them
The optimum of which they're capable.

The same might be said of the rhythm sections
In jazz combos: They drive the soloists
To intensities and explanations
Beyond even the formidable goals
Envisioned at the outset.

Hence, consider the sidemen
That Louie, Diz, Miles, and Coltrane
Surrounded themselves with
Once they had earned the luxury
Of being allowed to pick and choose.

Consider as well the vocalists, accompanists,
Conductors, arrangers, and instrumentalists,
Hand-picked by Frank Sinatra.
(Not to mention his bodyguard.)

Incomparability

The constants on all takes
Of the CD version of *Giant Steps*
Are the Jazz Giants: John Coltrane
On tenor sax, and Paul Chambers on bass.

But various of the main and alternate takes
Feature, on piano, Tommy Flanagan, Cedar
Walton, and Wynton Kelly, and, on drums,
Jimmy Cobb, Lee Humphries, and Art Taylor.

It is possible to analyze intelligently stylistic
Differences among these instrumentalists,
But it is the Quest of a Fool to attempt to
Rank or compare them in terms of excellence.

Similarly, let's not worry about whether
Bird, Sonny, or Trane
Was the greatest saxophonist,
Louis, Diz, or Miles, the best on trumpet.
Just thank God for all of them.

And anyway, are we counting in
The cornet and the flugelhorn?

Helen Lundeborg: *Plant and Animal Analogies*, 1934-35

Modernistic medical attempts
To improve upon the medieval artists
In the rendering of Madonna and Child
Fall as far short of the Masterpieces in the Getty,
As Joyce Kilmer did James Joyce,

As Madonna the Pseudo-Whore does the *Stabat Mater,*

As a comic strip does Raphael's *Cartoons,*

As Da Vinci sometimes does Da Vinci,

As *Game of Thrones* does the Topless Towers of Ilium.

something to hang on to

the day i turned sixty
i was late to the Y
for my swim
and i knew i'd have to make up for it
with a few sets on the exercise machines.
the weight room was filled with teenagers.
i swigged half a diet pepsi
and quipped to the desk girl,
"i guess i'd better show these whippersnappers
how a real man handles the heavy weights.

they seemed like nice kids
and a cross section of diversity,
but of course they couldn't hide their smiles
when i ambled in,
gray, gaunt, and wizened,
in tee shirt and jeans, and
against the posted rules,
birkenstocks.

and i won't claim that i can lift
as i did at thirty-five,
when i was a hundred pounds heavier
and not all of it beer,
or that i don't have to be careful these days
about popping a gut
or putting my spine into traction,

but when i saw their amusement
i made a point of adding twenty pounds
to the weight i found each machine at.

i didn't break any records,
not even my personal senior bests,
but by the time i retrieved my gym bag
and meandered casually back out to the lobby

the kids weren't chuckling anymore
but glad to see that there was hope for them
in those years so unimaginably far off
which will arrive as mine did
tomorrow.

Make Of This What You Will

At the Ellsworth Kelly exhibition
I observe a middle-aged man,
seemingly neither businessman or aesthete,
staring at one of the monumental
monochromatic biomorphic canvasses

with his eyes closed.

who's who

in the one-volume
encyclopedia of the twentieth century,
pablo picasso is "widely regarded as the
greatest visual artist of the century."
but, on the next page, the entry for
mary pickford is three times as long.

the common reader

an editor sends back
some poems of mine,
says he'd rather have some
   for "the common man."

i know what he means:
he'd rather have some from
my drinking days than ones that
contemplate and spring from
works of art.

yet, i know i'm nothing if not
common, now as in the past,
and i wonder why the worker must
be seen as relegated to the barroom,
the ennui that has been made of
sports on television, the commercial
interruptions, marketing research,
the bloat of coors and bud.

do we have so low an opinion
of the common man that we assume
he is not capable of appreciating
aaron copland, john cage, mahler,
hopper and van gogh.
poets other than bukowski,
rabbit angstrom,
death of a salesman,
stranger than paradise?

my friend, your heart is in
the right place but i think you
underrate the human potential.
when i lived in the bars, the
guys from the steam plant read
my chapbooks, passed them

around. sometimes came to
readings, sometimes still do,

and yeah, some of my poems
from those days celebrated pool
and pickled eggs, beef jerky and
baseball games, as well they should
have, but not all of them: others
dealt with honor, death, betrayal,
the *verismo* tragicomedy.

the common man of my day
has either died or is like me.
i think that he still understands my poems,
or could, if you'd give him the chance.
(if he looks up *verismo* it may lead him to
pagliacci and *cavalleria rusticana*—
check out *godfather three.*)

the common man of your age
is in college.

John Hoppner: *The Ladies Sarah and Catherine Bligh,* circa 1790

The slightly older, more muscular,
And less pretty Lady Catherine
Rests a protective or, perhaps,
Possessive hand upon the shoulder of
Lady Sarah, who seems somewhat
Sadly resigned to it.

I have no doubt that lesbianism
Was no less common in those days
Than today, when it seems quite
In vogue, but I wonder how often
It occurs between close siblings today,
Or did in those courtly times.
I'd be surprised if it were not at least
Dabbled in—tried out—in all times
And places, given the proximity of
The temptations and the opportunities
For privacy enjoyed upon spacious estates.

Frankly, I hope they were all doing it,
Just for the stimulation and since
Life without sex can be
Even more boring
Than life with it.

Jackson Pollock: *Untitled,* 1945

Beneath the randomness
Of sticks, snails, and scribbles,
May be discerned
Mutilated body parts.

What lengths we go to,
To express and then distance ourselves from
The perversities that excite us.

Why do you think so many works
Are left untitled?

To allow the viewer to make them
His/her own?

Yes, but also to pretend they are not
Mine or yours.

a teacher's idea of paradise

i'm about to check out of a hotel
much more comfortable than i ever
could afford for myself,
after a weekend's moonlighting for
a national testing service.
and i'm wishing I had one more day,
just on my own,
to read, write, swim, walk the grounds,
eat well, sleep well, free of all
responsibilities and deadlines . . .

maybe two days,
maybe a week . . .
would a month be unreasonable,
the rest of the summer downright greedy,
a year or two . . . ?

and every colleague that i share
this thought with
simply sighs.

henry's gift

my swedish friend,
henry demander,
whom i've never met,
sends me a zoot sims CD
from 1984 with the suggestion,
"put it on and forget about
your busy day at the university."

because he doesn't send me
the liner notes or album cover
i can't get all involved in trying to
expand my limited technical and
historical knowledge of this music
that i love so much.
"easy listening but a wonderfully
relaxing album," he adds, and he's right,
i do find time to just sit back and listen,
and i do relax, do nothing else,
let my mind wander as I might under the
massage of a long, hot shower.

our enemies are blowing up our buildings, and
would like to blow our bridges too.
anthrax is in the air.
small pox wants to come back from the dead
and spoil my pretty face.
saddam and bin laden would like
to go ballistic,
every time i turn on CNN,
i get uptight,
but i can't leave it off because
i might be the last guy in town
to learn of an evacuation order.

maybe that would be best anyway.
that's how zoot's strophes make me feel,

as mellow as lingonberry pancakes,
as absolutely laid-back as *absolut*,
as sane as dear old stockholm,
that the jazz guys love to serenade,
as cool as the west coast school.

i take zoot's gentle stylings into
sleep with me and, in the morning,
to my noontime swim at the ymca.

what a good friend henry is.
what good friends i have all over the country,
all over the world.

changing of the guard

when i enter the exercise room
at the local ymca
it is vacant.
i step on the treadmill, punch in weight,
distance, starting speed,
and begin to stroll.
gradually i increase my pace.
as i near my goal
i am moving along at a pretty good clip
and feeling so athletic and rejuvenated
that, just as the minute of cooling-down
clicks in, i rattle off a loud, healthy
machine-gun burst of flatulence.
what the hell—who's to hear?
and i'm leaving anyway.

i turn to find myself
face-to-face with an obese lady
who must have just slipped in
and alighted on the seat of the fly machine.
a new face; a first-timer.

"all yours," i smile,
and make my exit,
hoping i have done my part
to discourage overuse of the facilities.

the missing ingredient

the young jazz pianist
wowing the packed room at
the strenuous solo concert
has dazzling technique,
absolute mastery of theory,
and a modest, winning demeanor.
he inhabits every style
from ragtime and stride
to modern and postmodern
through a repertoire that embraces
"ain't misbehavin'," "they can't
take that away from me," and "misty."
no one has ever played more notes per second
with never a dull innovation.
he is eminently listenable,
and we are not talking some variety
of cocktail music.
he is some kind of genius.

he is also impeccably attired.
he is some mother's perfect son.
the audience, in fact, except for me,
seems to be wall-to-wall beverly hills,
slumming on behalf of a favorite son.
and yet something is lacking.

how to put it?
It's like the most brilliant
graduation recital
in the history of piano lessons.
it's as if george gershwin had been born
a performer instead of a composer.
it's that one gifted musical mimic
in every high school class
who is *de rigeur* at every class event,
a stylist raised here to the nth degree.

miles and chet didn't have
a tenth of his virtuosity.

A Still from *Diary of a Country Priest*

His cloak is as stark
As the barren, wintry trees,
His breath as dumb as farm animals
Who live to die.

He isolates himself in celibacy
For a silent god.

To be both priest and poet,
As Gerard Manley Hopkins was,
Is to double one's despair
(As if we weren't our own
Understudies to begin with).

The chromatic is black/gray
Though our dream craves Technicolor.

The music is ringing in the ears.

Some souls know only one season,
And some singers but one song.

Bun Eater, photo, Nilserik Larson, *Slipstream,* #33

Four men are being photographed
In a food court
But only one stares back
At the camera.

The other three are forfeiting
Their Fifteen Minutes
Of Meaninglessness.

an item from manila

"imelda marcos, 69, said her husband
was not a thief and amassed his fortune
through gold trading."

yeah, gold teeth.

ancient music

this bright, creative, dadaistic
high-school honors student
tells me that he's seen
the diego rivera exhibit in l.a.
we agree about its highlights,
but that you still have to go south
to view the monumental murals.

suddenly he adds,
"but he was so hideous . . .
and he was such a womanizer!"

so young, and already the feminists
have gotten their claws into him.

i'm tempted to tell him,
"kid, don't let the ladies tell you
what a man should look like
or how he should conduct
his affairs of the heart or
other organs."

but he'll have to hear it
either in my poems
or in his blood.

timing is everything

the horoscope this morning
really put me on my guard,
sent the adrenalin coursing
through my veins,
as it predicted a crucial confrontation
that would require all the will and
ingenuity that i could muster . . .

until i remembered i was looking at
a week-old student newspaper.

the lyrics linger on

for my 60th birthday
i decided to treat myself
to spaghetti and meatballs,
a childhood favorite,
although i don't eat much meat anymore.
but i dicked around
with this and that,
walking the dog,
shoveling the cat box,
until, by the time i got to joe ferrara's
great calabrian restaurant,
the families were lined up for tables
out onto the heated patio.
so i started down wardlow
until i came to a little place
i'd just about forgotten about.
but it was under new management
and expanded into two art deco dining rooms
and was called an "italian bistro" now
and the spaghetti and meatballs cost
four bucks more than at guiseppe's
and the meatballs tasted like shit,
worse than soybean,
more like ground squirrel or 'possum
or something bought in bulk at costco.
the waitresses were very attractive, though,
and attentive, as they might as well have been,
since for a while i was the only diner there.
and this black guy of indeterminate age
was at an old piano playing and singing
old songs, most of which i didn't even recognize,
and he couldn't sing for shit,
and he couldn't play for shit,
and he seemed wired on something
stronger than caffeine,
but just as the check arrived

i realized that he was playing "lazy bones,"
a tune my aunts had used
to urge me gently out of bed
when i was maybe three years old:
"lazy bones, sleepin' in the sun,
how you gonna get your day's work done . . .

and when he goes a fishin',
lazy bones' a-whishin'
that the fish won't bite . . ."

when the song was over—
clever lyrics but too politically incorrect
for media performance nowadays
with their implication that plantation negroes
were living the life of riley—

i pulled a couple of wrinkled dollars
out of my pocket for his tip jar
and said, "it's been a long time
since i heard that song,
a *long* time, maybe fifty-seven years,"

and he just grinned . . . maybe he had been
passing it off as an original composition.

no matter: "lazy bones" was a nice surprise
for a guy celebrating,
or mourning,
his 60th birthday,
with the last of his doting aunts
recently passed away.
it almost made up for
the disappointment of
that overpriced platter of
utterly un-italian
spaghetti and meatballs.

I Give Up, or I Want My Sixty Bucks Back

After writing eleven or twelve
Half-way decent poems
Contemplating the first (and best)
Eleven or Twelve prints
In the catalog of
The Surrealist Adventures of Women Artists
In Mexico and the United States,
a.k.a. *In Wonderland,*

The poet pages through
The rest of the book
Four Times
Before concluding that
Great Literature cannot by inspired by
Pedestrian Art.

Grand-Madonna and Child

When our daughter's first child was born,
Eight months ago,
I was overjoyed for her,
And, as for myself, well, my attitude
Has always been, "the more, the merrier."

I knew my wife was really looking forward to this,
More than she would let on,
But I had no idea that it would be the start
Of a whole new life for her.
She has practically abducted the kid.
That's an exaggeration—she is third in line,
After the mother and father,
But as I tell people: She is running
A VERY STRONG THIRD!

This summer, for instance, she rises at 5:00 a.m.
To wake up gradually
And drive half an hour each way to babysit
From 7:15 a.m. to 6:00 p.m. so the parents,
Their parental leave exhausted,
Can return to their jobs.
She grabs a breakfast snack,
Packs a lunch, and arrives home too late for me
To take her out for dinner.
It's a Second Motherhood for her,
Bottles and baby food, diapers, tidying
Laundry, quick reads during naps,
Daily outings on walks or to the park,
By stroller or car seat, with the happy dog
Always on its best behavior.

When I ask how it's going, she confesses
All the little indications that her grandson is
The sweetest, cutest, brightest little boy,
Since her own kids were born.

We've been together over forty years
And we have, to put it as mildly as baby lotion,
Had our occasional differences—like constantly,
But I've never wished her unhappiness,
Although I've certainly contributed to it.
Still, I never would have guessed
That she could ever have found herself
This happy, this ecstatic, this fulfilled,
This transformed, this redeemed,
Again.

No Free Lunch

The cat on the back of the sofa
Watching the birds and squirrels
Feed and frolic on the patio
Outside the sliding glass window,

Realizes he is living his life
In a cage
Only slightly larger than that
Of the parakeet.

Courtesy of his loving (themselves) owners,
Who have bought his freedom
From the pet shop or pound,
He has been further relieved of the burdens
Of procreation and child-rearing,
While being afforded a waived tuition
Into what Bunuel nailed as
The Discreet Charms of the Bourgeoisie.

Francis Picabia: *Alarm Clock*, 1919

It is the cover illustration
Of *DADA 4-5*,
The reduction to absurdity
That was said to have been short-lived,
And quickly subsumed into Surrealism,
But within my lifetime re-emerged
In the pages of Marvin Malone's
Storied *Wormwood Review*,
And in the games of "Ubu Pool"
At which Kirk Robertson and I
Would improvisationally Anti-Compete
Upon the tattered puke-green felt,
Of the minimalist pool table
Blocking the aisle of the Forty-Niners Tavern
Where DADA was the lifestyle,
Undefined but pre-determined,
For the undermining of all pious utterances
Choked from the collective exhaust manifolds
Of the passing traffic on the PCH,
Outside the bolted after-hours no-exit-entrances
Of this spontaneous and audience-inclusive
Temple/Fortress of God's Own Performance of
His inspired and inspiring Disappearance Act.

The Toad Solution

Mrs. Toad says to Mr. Toad:
"Well, the second row of garage lights
Has gone out now. So we have
No lights at all in the garage anymore,
Which is, by the way, where,
Among other necessities,
Our washer and dryer are located.

"Can you replace the bulbs?" Toad asks.

"Not without breaking my neck."

"Do we have any kind of handyman on retainer
We could call to replace them?"

"I guess you haven't noticed but, actually,
We haven't had a regular handyman
In at least ten years, only a contractor
Who will delegate the biggest, most expensive jobs,
And *you* certainly aren't either handyman or contractor."

"I've never aspired," Toad says, "to those vocations,
Let alone avocations—I am a Musician
Of the English Language . . . but I will tell you what
Would be the first step I would take
If I considered any such steps to fall under
The rubric of my responsibilities."

"Let me guess: You'd get out
The Yellow Pages."

"No, my dear, I'd check to see
If our flashlight needed batteries."

Huxley's Soma

When I run into students of mine
From the 1960s or '70s
Who promote marijuana as a harmless,
Perhaps even healthful,
Alternative to alcohol,
And who sneered at the statistical suggestion
That it led to harder drugs,
And who have now seen their utopian dream
Of medicinal or decriminalized dope
Outlast the attempts at prohibition,
And I ask them how their literary,
Musical, professional, or monetary
Ambitions have panned out,

I see them looking back into themselves
For the answers,
Just as they did in classrooms
Fifty years ago,
Oblivious to lectures,
Or as they sat in silence at parties
That had once been social occasions.

My Fifteen Seconds of Fame

When I was much younger
And had a big black beard
And long black hair,
If I went to Tijuana,
I heard, "Hey, Fidel!"

And at the Top Dog in Berkeley,
Someone would call, "I know you-you're
Jerry Garcia!"

And once at a hamburger stand
Off Highway One in Lucia,
A woman called me
The Illegitimate Son of Mr. Madman
(Which became a chapbook of mine
From Slipstream Press),

So I think I can be forgiven,
Now that I'm in my seventies,
If someone on the street will occasionally
Ask me, "Aren't you Gerry Locklin?"

And it will occur to me that,
For what it's worth,
I actually am.

Olfactory Poetics

As soon as I get a whiff
Of "poetry" in a poem
(Not excluding my own),

I strongly suspect
It isn't one.

The Wedding of Tyler and Nicole

They say Nobody's Perfect,
And they say there's no such thing
As a Perfect Match,
But the day Tyler and Nicole tied the knot,
God and Darwin were doing lunch,
And God said, "Well, I sure got it right
This time—you'll have to grant me
That one, Chucky-baby! They're like
The wind in the waves,
The perfect lyric for a flawless melody,
The paradoxically equinoctial solstice."

But Darwin said, "Wait a minute, Big Guy,
I made this match, though I'll admit
It took me many an eon of trial and error,
Hit and miss."

So they were off and running once again,
As ongoing an argument as
Hegel's idealistic dialectic
Versus Marx's materialistic one,

Whereas the simple, silly fact was that
They'd always ended up with pretty much
The same old universe anyway, just viewed
From celestial or temporal vantages,

And this time, yes, they'd mutually arrived at,
In the marriage of Tyler and Nicole,
A collaboration about as perfect as
The intervals of the Fibonacci Sequence,

And the Golden Ratio.

A Formerly Omniscient Toad

His students used to say
That Professor Toad knew everything.

They were right.

And he still does.

He just can't remember any of it.

The Consequences of Childhood/Adolescent Deprivations

W.C. Fields felt it necessary
During his years of greatest success
To open bank accounts in nearly every town at which
His train laid over long enough for him to do so.
He never wanted to be caught without cash again,
Not to know where his next meal was coming from.
It's said that in his later years he could no longer recall
Where all those greenback hordes were stashed.
I wonder if back then inactive funds escheated
To the state eventually, as they do today.
At any rate, it's surmised that his executors
Never did track down all those acorns that
He'd sacked away for a rainy day.

Toad felt as an adult
That he had lots of wasted time and spilt sperm
To catch up on, to make up for.
Even when quite happy with a wife or mistress,
Sometimes passionately so,
He found it necessary to stockpile
Understudies for their roles.
Via flirtatious conversations,
Correspondence, or meaningful embraces,
He sought to convey his potentially serious intentions,
And when he closed his letters, "Affectionately,"
"Warmly," "Love," or "Yours,"

He hoped to signal to them that they were indeed
Moving up the depth chart.

Grace Plethorpe: *Ancestors, II,* 1935, Ink

Yes, we carry in every cell
Nuanced imagery not only of the caveman
But of the species and unicellular microorganisms
Which constitute our true genetic histories.

Thus, the eyes and mouths and intestines,
The ova and the spermatozoa,
That squirm and worm and finger their way
Even into our ostensibly sophisticated
Impulses, preferences, motivations,
Grand decisions, and performances
(And delusions).
Look at that rooster's eye!
Behold the dragon's teeth,
The snarky, sharky bloodthirst,
The gasping loneliness,
The urge to devour or poison the mate,
The flattened face emerging from
The streamlined frontal lobe.

We are ourselves a frottage, a garbage can,
A boneyard, and a Sargasso sandwich.
No wonder when we orgasm,
We sometimes, simultaneously, shit.

A Momentary Mental Lapse

When Toad announced to his wife
That he was toying with accepting
An invitation to participate in
A four-day bilingual poetry festival
In Tijuana
In spite of being in the midst of
A battery of medical tests
That had begun in the Emergency Ward,

Her succinct response was,
Are you fucking nuts?

Later he consulted his girlfriend
In regard to the same invitation.
Are you, she inquired,
Out of your fucking mind?

The deciding factor, however,
Was a viewing of the film, *Savages*.
And when he called the local Spanish professor
Who had conveyed the invitation,
To beg off for reasons of health,
He discovered that this previous enthusiast
Had not much stomach for going to the festival either
All by his lonesome.

No Green Berlin

In my memory of a few days in Berlin,
There is no green.
A Molecule Man stands tall
In the River Spree, but molecules are not
Holes; real men eschew high heels;
And neither polio nor panzer divisions
Assault us in our time.

Every metropolis has its Hauptbahnhof,
Its stately bustling Central Station,
But beautiful buildings cannot be held
Responsible for the uses to which they are put.

Berlin beckons us to the self-igniting flame
Of the Crystal Cupola on the New Reichstag,
Like the bare, skeletal gams of Marlene Dietrich.

Potsdamer Platz is not Potsdam,
(Though Potsdam isn't either).
The trenchant faces of its trilogy of buildings
Are a post-human Carnival of Triangulating Circuitries:
You enter the matrix and emerge a lesser person.

The Bode Museum on Museum Island
Bears witness to Postmodern Capitals as
Museums of Themselves.

The poster of a Russian soldier at Checkpoint Charlie:
So young, so young, to be the cruel captain of Purgation.

The Twin Towers and identical ticket booths
Of Olympic Stadium exhibit a fashionable functionality.
Only the paving stones of the parking lots
Are irregularly cracked, perhaps by Der Fuhrer's Rage
For and against the future Jesse Owens augured.

The Christmas Market at the
Kaiser Wilhelm Memorial Church:
Who would ever want to forget
Kaiser Bill, Kaiser Billie?

New buildings built within the ruins of Old:
As with Coventry and Cordoba, it can be a
Great idea, but the New Synagogue on
Oranienburger Strasse may present
A slightly too inviting target.

Oh My God: between the small reflecting pool
And the Red Town Hall and Television Tower
I can't deny that I discern a minimal strip of lawn.
I bet it has been planted in the last ten years, which have
Seen Germany become the creditor of the European Union.
Maybe even in honor of Greenback Dollars
And Daddy Warbucks. But how rich is any creditor
If his debtors will never afford to pay him back?

Walking to the Cultural Center constructed from
A brewery in the former East Berlin, I note the
Cafés full of aspiring writers, artists, intellectuals—
Most, I am told, on the dole—also aging pensioners
In their aging apartment buildings, desecrated with
Left-wing graffiti. I am patronizingly assured
The audience is fluent beyond belief in English, but
That proves not to extend to my vernacular ironies,
Sarcasms, and ambiguities. I spend most of my mic-time
Singing Sinatra and Streisand, tap-dancing, and soaring
Ceilingward (well, a few inches anyway) like
The World's Oldest Male Peter Pan, the oldest
Female being Cathy Rigby.

I've forgotten what or how many victories are
Celebrated by the Victory Column. Those of
Vercingetorix? Wasn't he Swiss? The trees and
Winged Victory loom black against the torrid sky.

Of course there is a famous zoo, a famous deer park:
Maybe the animals are painted green. Maybe they are
Cannons in camouflage. I do not visit them.
I don't sample the renowned nightlife decadence,
Because I'm watching over my daughter,
Less than a year after 9/11, who will commence
The Turning Point of Law School in the fall.
She is invisibly and invariably green of heart
And always will be. Others may be green with envy,
Who need not be, who have earned their own
Inviolable laurels and inestimable love.

What have I learned from Berlin? That
Fascism and Communism and Unrestrained
Capitalism all combat the vernal culmination
Of renewal, suck the green from memory.
Your memories of Berlin may be more colorful;
My mental palate may have been in atrophy.
And of all cities it's the one I most long to
Revisit, for a longer stay, alone, perhaps,
To quaff my fix of Weimar Blue Angelic,
And then go to hell.

A Green Thought?

Andrew Marvell is best known for
His seductively detailed, syllogistically argued
Plea "To His Coy Mistress,"
The Carpe Diem to end all Carpe Diems.
But in graduate school we were instructed
To appreciate as well the elusive, ineluctable
Analyses of Mind (Human and or Universal?)
That constitute this polar removal from the External,
Or Mirror of It: "The Garden." And to admire it
As including perhaps the most musically
Beautiful and enigmatic couplet in English Verse:
"Annihilating all that's made
To a green thought in a green shade."

Ever the pedagogue, I'll suggest the poem
Anticipates by two centuries the *"ineffable,"*
And the "correspondences" between the Visible World
And the Ocean of Thought of the French Symbolists—
Nerval, Baudelaire, Verlaine, Rimbaud, Mallarmé, Laforgue,
Corbière, Valéry, and arguably, Apollinaire,
And of our own Edgar Allan Poe, T.S. Eliot,
Hart Crane, and Wallace Stevens, not to mention,
A sequence of major, cross-disciplinary movements
That partially derived from them: Futurism, Dadaism,
Surrealism (Freudian, then Marxist), and
L-A-N-G-U-A-G-E.

But, like a lazy Socrates, I'll also let you
Discover or revisit for yourselves the Many Mansions
Of this philosophical inquiry in nine stanzas
Of eight lines of four stresses each,
Into the nature of the consciousness
And of the Green World which may exist either
Within it or outside it or as simply with it:
A single Green Thought in a Green Shade,
Or a Boundless Master-Matrix-Molecule of Many.

The Secret to My Success

I read in *Time* magazine
How blue became the "signature color"
For Yves Klein, how it symbolized
Not only "the eternal," but
"Somehow the gateway for entering it."

I guess having a signature color,
Especially BLUE,
(Let's not forget *Blue Boy* or
Picasso's BLUE PERIOD)
Can help an artist achieve wealth and fame.

That gave me the idea
Of attempting something similar,
But since I work with sounds,
I decided I would have to use
Not a signature color,
But a SIGNATURE SYLLABLE.

How's this one:

"DUH, DUH, DUH, DUH,
DUH, DUH, DUH . . ."

the silence

in *rituals*, by cees noteboom,
a character speaks of the "wonderful silence"
that a nuclear catastrophe would bring.

no one in truth desires that,
but i can understand
the longing inspired by the concept.

it's new year's but i don't
turn on the rose bowl yet.
i don't turn on the countdown
of the greatest jazz hits
on the greatest jazz station,
KLON.
even this writing is a sort of inner noise
not altogether joyful.

solitary confinement is one of the hells;
the voices of the schizophrenic are another.

i cherish this hour
in a deafened cosmos of the mind,
but only for as long
as i am not condemned to it.

Orthographic Depths in Secret Gardens

Toad wonders:

What is the semantic relationship
Between
Genomes and Gnomes?!

Cryptography

Until Toad attended
The Imitation Game,

He assumed it involved
The snapshots by tourists

Of the tombs of
Royalty, Poets, and Pederasts

In the vaults of Westminster Abbey.

Who the hell greenlighted it?

Kim Jung Un III,
Ruler of North Korea,
Might have shown a little leniency
To the cyber-circuits of SONY

If he hadn't found
The Interview
As big a waste of his time
As did those millions of Americans
Who never, among them, uttered
A single giggle.

Nothing Special Anymore

Toad had always assumed
He would one day make
A return trip to Cuba,
Where he'd enjoyed
A Hemingway Symposium
In the summer of 1997,

Until Obama decreed
He was going to allow
Every Tom, Jose, and Hairy Dick
Not only to visit the fabled isle
And sample its cigars, rums, and
Sugar cane,

But, for a nominal fee,
Take a guided tour of Guantanamo
And, when the tides were right,
Try their hands (and feet and faces)
At their choice of either surfboarding
Or waterboarding.

From Gloat to Goat

His first time back to
Plant-watering duties
Subbing for his wife
While she spent the days
Babysitting their one-and-two-year-old
Grandchildren, he thought he had caught her
In a major, literal faux pas
When he discovered she had left
The faucet of the front-yard water valve
In the Open Position.

Stepping away from it, however,
With hose in hand,
He heard beneath his sodden Birkenstocks
The crunching of one of the hundred or so
Tiny bulbs of the Christmas Lights
Strung along the bricks enclosing
Their Garden of Succulents.

He hoped she was exaggerating
That every last one of them
Would be rendered dark and smoky,

But his best friend at the donut shop
Assured him that he had
Ruined not only his own,
But very possibly
Every damn source of holiday cheer
For the surrounding twenty or so
Square miles.

Thumbnail Guide for the Senior Couplers

No matter how you coupled,
If you coupled at all.
And if it was fun while you were doing it,
And you came (or close) at the end of it,
Who cares who was putting what into whom.
Where, or how many times?

These and many other details are INESSENTIAL!!!
Maybe it was just a damn fine backrub!!!
It's not even ESSENTIAL that there be a next time.
It's more ESSENTIAL that you retain a memory
Of THIS TIME . . . and even a SENSE MEMORY
Of SOMETHING HAVING HAPPENED
Will suffice.

As far as the next time is concerned,
Well, you've earned a next time,
But then again, we don't always get to cash
Our final pension checks in either.

And, anyway, was there ever a time in our lives
When, man or woman,
LGBT or straight, we knew for sure
Where our next piece of ass was coming from,
Or even IF one was? And, as anyone will tell you:
The worst piece of ass you ever had,
Was probably not all THAT BAD either!
And who knows, maybe we take our memories with us,
Except up there, they're not just dreams, they're
Like a porno film in which we star eternally,
And God's a smiling, ageless popcorn-popping
Pharmacist, distributing these little blue pills.

I Hate Hollywood

I hate its blockbusters.
I hate its expensive blockbuster theaters.
I hate its parking problems.
I hate its potholes.
I hate its drug dealers, and
I hate their customers.
I hate its gang mentality.
I hate its rip-off apartments and motels and restaurants.
I hate its clubs, but I love its cemeteries.
I hate its lack of loyalty, and
I hate its rip-off royalties.
I hate the way its kids are raised.
I hate everything old about it, and
I hate everything new.
I hate the way everyone votes
For the same people,
And then votes to recall them.
I hate its celebrities who try to be poets, and
I hate its poets who aspire to be celebrities.
I hate its hypocrisies, and
I hate its theocracies.
I hate everything Fitzgerald, Faulkner,
West, and Hemingway hated about it.
I hate what it did or tried to do to Bukowski.
I hate its ersatz Bukowskians.
I hate the Hollywood Sign, the Hollywood Bowl,
The Hollywood Bowling Alleys, the Hollywood
Hills and the Hollywood Canyons, and
I do not discriminate in my hatred of all
Its residents of any race, and all its tourists
Who stare at the Chinese Theater, and I hate
The homeless who mug them and murder them,
But I applaud that they burn down each other's

Homes and businesses and flatten each other's
Tires. I even hate things that are non-existent,
Such as its entire infrastructure, whose pipes burst
Every day because they didn't have a dollar spent
On them in 100 delusional years.
Obviously, I don't hate its earthquakes.
I don't hate Ed Ruscha's painting of a
Hollywood Sunset, behind a Hollywood sign,
Which means the sun is somehow setting in the North,
I don't hate Randy Newman because if you read
Between the lines he hates Los Angeles, also.
I hate those foolish drivers who lead police
On car chases and then are surprised when
They are rewarded with cracked skulls.
I have adrenal glands also, lots of them.

Maybe I should admit that Hollywood seduced
The love of my life away from me,
But I am too sophisticated,
As you can see, to allow
That to jaundice
My urbane appraisal of
The Woods of Holly.

Gustave Moreau: *Oedipus and the Sphinx*, 1864

She plants her lioness's feet
High on his thighs, as her claws
Tear at his cloak and bindings.
Everything above her wings is pointed:
Nose, lips, chin, and nipples,
Desperately rising towards his gaze
And features, matched to hers,
And only a flash from locking
With her own desire's species-defying
Immolation. He not only would kill for her,
But already has, and the fire of their
Mutually lustful seductions will move
The clouds to move the crags they
Lean against.

You sure have to hand it to those crazy
Greeks and their apprenticed French
Romance interpreters. They sure knew how
To turn a simple fuck into an epic.

Dieric Bouts: *Virgin and Child,* 1455-60

The divine kid already knew
How to tease a woman's lips
With peripheral kisses:

But then, why wouldn't He?
He was the same God
Who'd invented genders, sex, and
Foreplay in the first place,
And he only had a few finite years
In which to try out how well
His elaborate eternally contemplated blueprint
For human procreation
Was working out in a society
That seemed hell-bent to fuck up
Even his most omniscient, omnipotent attempts
At getting a few Goddamned things right.

Camille Pisarro: *The Garden of the Tuileries on a Spring Morning*, **1899**

He'd studied trigonometry
With his friend Cézanne,
But he hadn't exiled from his gardens
The progeny of Adam and Eve.

Colum Colvin: *Cupid and Psyche*, 1986

Even a third-quarter (and third-rate) cubist
Covering the upper chest with a rectangular text,
Could not entirely destroy the riveting power
Of a woman—any woman—in the vise of passion.

Vincent Van Gogh: *The Flowering Orchard* **and**
Claude Monet: *Fruit Trees in Blossom*

Today's quiz question is,
Whose tree seems
More in the throes of either
Electrocution or a severe anxiety attack?

And whose is just happy
To be defrosting?

Maybe at Heart

The counter girl at the Corner Mexican Restaurant
Takes my order of One Cheese Enchilada,
One Shrimp Taco, One Grilled Fish Taco,
One order of chips, and one small Diet Pepsi,

And says, "Monday is Senior Discount Day, sir:
How old are you?"

"Seventy-three," I say.

"What?!" she says.

I repeat my age.

"Oh," she says, and smiles:
"I thought you were trying to tell me
That you're only seventeen."

Pablo Picasso: *Seated Harlequin*, **1901**

When the harlequin sits,
He overthinks the situation.
Even alcohol may become
The depressant it's always been.

A posture may become a pensive pose.
Suddenly the wallpaper may seem
As deadly boring as it's always been.
The petals *of Les Fleurs du Mal*
Have ceased to be poetic fun.

O, Carlos, when did your countenance
Pale to the pallor of *symboliste* impertinence,
Your paragraph bordered by periods,
And blue no longer the warmest tint?

Be careful what you wish for, Mr. Blue:
You may become your affectations,
Your death an elegiac inspiration,
Oft doth the artist outlive his muses.

Henri Matisse: *Icarus*, **Plate Vii of** *Jazz*, **1947**

Beware the soaring of the spirit!
Beware elating aspirations!
Those golden stars, seductive
To the Over-Reacher, may be
False positives of premature demises.
There is no swimming in the secret sea,
The spirituous a distant cousin of the spirit.
Man was not meant to walk on waterways.
Our winged destiny is doomed to melt
In the plummeting of the planetary exile.
Black Beauty turns momentary in the
Immolating, cerulean, ecstasy.

Van Gogh did not survive *Starry Night*.

Paul Cézanne: *Still Life with a Ginger Jar and Eggplants,* 1893-94

Eggplants are the vegetative earth.
They are also an excellent substitute
For meats, especially when baked
In the manner of Parma.
Some perceive them as uncomfortably fleshy
And are troubled by that.
But adjust or perish.

The water pot speaks for its essential self.
The ginger jar adds spice to life,
The gigolo of the kitchen.
The smaller fruits are sometimes peachy
And sometimes tartly citric. Life requires
A balanced pH Factor, marital adjustment
Of the acidic and the alkaline,
The cloth suggests our intestinal complexities,
Complexity Theory itself, meant to render
Chaos Measurable and Manageable.
Thank God for the A to Z—Antacids to Zantac—
Of our pharmacopeia. In the window,
A hairy stick-figure observes the domesticity
That sometimes makes and sometimes un-makes
Him and Her. P.S. The art is color, line, and structure,
Maybe just a whisper of texture to require
A pittance for an Endowed Lecturer.

Hippopotamus: **Egypt**

"William, the Unofficial Mascot of the Met"
Is said to represent "fertility, rebirth, and
The Goddess Hathor, Lady of Turquoise."

He seems to me an embodiment of Playfulness,
The freedom enjoyed by an ancient sense of fun
That may have been the Birth of Art from Recreation,
Respite from the unremitting watchfulness required
Just to stay alive in the midst of an endemic of
Perishing species, the casualties of
Pre-sentimental Evolution.

Humanity has always had to kill to live,
Much as that is mocked these days,
And civilizing inclinations are
Its own worst enemies, probably imprinted by some
Mysterious Fibonaccian Genomic Looping
Of into Extinction/Re-sequencings.

Filippino Lippi: *Madonna and Child,* 1483-84

The Immaculate Conception and the Virgin Birth:
Miracle of Miracles! Let us all give praise and,
As with the Host, Swallow it!

To tell the truth,
My belief in miracles and the divine
Is constantly renewed.
To augment Pascal's Wager,
One need only add that
God created Evolution
And continues to.
It's no more difficult to buy into
The latter of the two
Than to conceptualize
Matter and energy without Beginning or End.

The Christ-Child is shown at play.
He's just like any other kid.
Enjoy yourself, guy: you'll have more
Than one cross to bear.

And those Romanesque arches in the background:
Do they represent the way we arch our backs
When playing our part in
The Miracle of Procreation?

"Doctor, I want a lens I can trust!"

When she insisted that her car
Had been parked all afternoon
In the driveway where his eyes
Had assured him,
No vehicle all day
Had been at rest,

Toad wondered if,
Should he ever catch her in bed
With a strange and naked man,
She would have the nerve to re-enact
The hallowed indignation of,

"There's no one in this bed except me!
You really need to get your eyes examined!"

Vincent Van Gogh: *Irises*, **1890**

His "blue period" was a pretty one,
A respite from both mania and depression,
A quietessence of normality.

He bequeathed the madness to a century
Of rocketry and auction houses.

George Woodall: *Vase*, late 19th Century

Her filmy, flimsy wind-blown garments
Fail to conceal the beauty of her naked flesh,
Especially when animated as dance,
The silently tinted breathtaking attraction
Of her physicality.

The Pre-Raphaelites reminded us
That creation and procreation
Are co-terminus and that
All art is religious.

Constantin Guys: *Young Woman in a Blue and Black Dress*

Her features, flesh, and expression
Show her to be
Composed of those colors
Always meant to suggest:

Sweets and spices and all of the niceties,

And some wonderful unmentionables
As well.

The Kindest Cut

When upon leaving her bed
At an earlier hour than she desired,
His mistress screamed of his marriage,

"You must live in a prison!"

The same unfairness that infuriated him
Also served to guarantee
That he would someday soon be asserting
An even greater freedom of movement

Away from both of them.

Andy Warhol: *Nice Jackies*, **1964**

Her single photo moves
Through stages of blue
To almost lifelike and
Beginning-to-vanish
Copper.

All things conspire
To comprise our destinies.

And our emotions are our experiencing
Of our colorations.

Diego Rivera: *The Flower Carriers*, **1935**

I don't know: better cotton candies
Than potatoes or pig iron.

But what the hell: it's all about
Diagonals, harmony, and balance
Anyhow.

a pathetic finale

y'know, it was only recently
that i read or heard
that apparently time-honored advice
for gaining confidence
in front of an audience
by imagining them naked.
both my wife and my students assured me
it was the oldest chestnut blackening
under the tree.

i warned my class that if
i were ever to fall into
an absentminded silent stare
in front of them, it should be taken
as merely a senior moment, not an act
of comprehensive sexual harassment
(no matter how broad the grin on my face).

but that night, at a melodramatic production
that left the entire cast in tears
it occurred to me that they might have achieved
this deep emotional verisimilitude
by imagining *me* naked.

Robert Colescott: *End of the Trail*, 1976

At the end of the trail,

the Indian gets the underwear,
the Adidas,
the brush/quill,

the white teeth,

and

the last laugh.

Acknowledgements

"Rembrandt: *The Polish Rider*, 1655" was published in *5am*; "Albrecht Dürer: *Adam and Eve*, 1504," "Hans-Christian Schink: *Autobahn Landscape*, photograph," and "Richard Diebenkorn: *Freeway and Snapshot*, 1957" were published in *Ambit;* "Honoré Daumier: *The Laundress*, 1863" was published on *Cadence Collective*; "From Gloat to Goat," "Nothing Special Anymore," and "Who the Hell Greenlighted It" were published in *Café Review*; "Double Call, photo, Nilserik Larson, *Slipstream*, #33," "Eileen Agar: *Ladybird*, 1936," "Giovanni di Paolo: *The Expulsion of Adam and Eve from Paradise*," "Karet Taipei: *Collage #45*, 1938," "Lauren Simonutti: *Bring the Candle to the Flame*, Slipstream Postcard," "Lorenzo Lotto: *Venus and Cupid*," and "*Memories of Madness*, photograph by Andrea Faseni, Front Cover, *Slipstream #33*" were published in *Carnival Literary Magazine*; "Agustin Lazo: *The Family Reunion*, ca. 1931," "A Momentary Mental Lapse," and "Grace Plethorpe: *Ancestors, II*, 1935, Ink" were published in *Free State Review*; "A Formerly Omniscient Toad" was published in *Home Planet News*; "Giant Steps," "Countdown," and "Spiral" were published in *Malpais Review*; "Eugene Berman: *Hugh and Bridget Chisholm*, 1940," "Francis Picabia: *Alarm Clock*, 1919," "Frida Kahlo: *Mi vestigo cuelga ahi (My dress hangs there)*, 1933," "Harmonizing over the Bar Lines," "Incomparability," "Lola Alvarez Bravo: *El sueño del ahogado*, c. 1945," "No Free Lunch," "The Toad Solution," and "Those Who Drive the Engine" were published in *Mas Tequila Review*; "Andy Warhol: *A Boy for Me*, 1962" and "Today's Avant-Garde go over the Hill Tomorrow" were published in *Milk*; "Helen Lundeborg: *Plant and Animal Analogies*, 1934-35," "I Give Up, or I Want My Sixty Bucks Back," "Lola Alvarez Bravo: *El sueño del ahogado (The Dream of the Drowned)*," and "Sir Anthony VanDyck: *Marchesa Giovanna Cattaneo*" were published in *Minotaur*; "Cindy Sherman: *Untitled #123*, 1983," "Huxley's Soma," "My Fifteen Seconds of Fame," "Olfactory Poetics," and "The Consequences of Childhood/Adolescent Deprivations" were published in *Nerve Cowboy*; "The Secret to My

Success" was published in *Over the Transom;* "a teacher's idea of paradise" and "the common reader" were published in *Pearl;* "Grand-Madonna and Child" and "Willem de Kooning: *Pink Angels,* 1945" were published in *Presa;* "a pathetic finale," "something to hang on to," and "timing is everything" were published in *Quercus Review;* "A Green Thought?" "No Green Berlin," and "The Winter Trees of Summer" were published by Silver Birch Press; "David Hockney: *Lithograph of Water Made of Thick and Thin Lines, a Green Wash, a Light Blue Wash and a Dark Blue Wash (Pool 1),* 1978-80, Lithograph in Seven Colors" and "John Singleton Copley: *Portrait of Elizabeth Ross (Mrs. William Tyng),* 1766" were published in *Slagdog;* "ancient music," "Jackson Pollock: *Untitled,* 1945," "John Hoppner: *The Ladies Sarah and Catherine Bligh,* circa 1790," "the lyrics linger on," and "Thumbnail Guide for the Senior Couplers" were published in *Slipstream;* "Matisse: *Le Bonheur de Vivre,* 1905-06," "*The Unicorn in Captivity,* Brussels, 1495-1505," and "The Wedding of Tyler and Nicole" were published in *Snail Mail Review;* "Grand Designs and Delusions of Grandeur," "Picasso: *Le Moulin de la Galette,* Winter 1900," "Picasso: *Woman Ironing,*" and "slide" were published in *Tears in the Fence*; "he reads; she beads," "Make Of This What You Will," and "those people who call other people paranoid" were published in *ZZZ Zyne.*

About the Author

Gerald Locklin has published over one hundred volumes of poetry, fiction, and literary essays including *Charles Bukowski: A Sure Bet*, (Water Row Press) and *Go West, Young Toad*, (Water Row Press). Charles Bukowski called him "One of the great undiscovered talents of our time." *The Oxford Companion to Twentieth Century Literature in the English Language* calls him "a central figure in the vitality of Los Angeles writing." His works have been widely translated and he has given countless readings here and in England. He is a Professor Emeritus at California State University, Long Beach. Visit Gerald Locklin's website at www.geraldlocklin.org.

www.ingramcontent.com/pod-product-compliance
Lightning Source LLC
Chambersburg PA
CBHW020940090426
42736CB00010B/1204